THE HANDS OF A GREAT LEADER

IT STARTS ON THE INSIDE

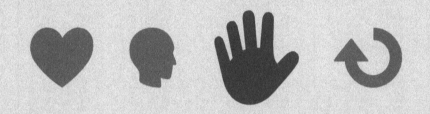

An in-depth study guide by

KEN BLANCHARD & PHIL HODGES

with STEVE GARDNER

LEAD LIKE JESUS

TABLE OF CONTENTS

OUR HOPE FOR YOU

WE WANT YOU TO EXPERIENCE JESUS IN A WHOLE DIFFERENT WAY — TO GROW TO TRUST HIM AS THE PERFECT ONE TO FOLLOW AS YOU SEEK TO LEAD OTHERS. THIS INVOLVES SURRENDERING OUR LIVES AND LEADERSHIP TO HIM.

The real secret to leading like Jesus is found in PROVERBS 3:5-6: *Trust in the Lord with all your heart and lean not on your own understanding; in all your ways acknowledge him, and he will make your paths straight.*

Jesus is clear about how He wants us to lead. He asks us to make a difference in our world by being effective servant leaders. It is our prayer and desire that this Lead Like Jesus *HANDS Study Guide* will be the beginning of a new and exciting chapter in your personal journey to becoming just that. It is designed to guide you in exploring your personal response to Jesus' call to *follow Me* and to put into action the principles of servant leadership.

Don't worry if you do not have a formal leadership role. The principles are applicable to your relationship with your spouse, kids, friends, coworkers, colleagues, and casual acquaintances. This isn't the intellectual pursuit of a complicated philosophy of leadership; it is a guide to a more practical application of the truths of Scripture. We want you to think differently, but we also want you to develop a lifestyle that is built upon and governed by your relationship with Jesus Christ — the ultimate leader!

STUDY GUIDE OVERVIEW

HOW THIS STUDY GUIDE IS DESIGNED

We have designed this guide for daily study so that the principles you learn can be consistently put to work in your daily life. The focus is your hands — your behavior as a leader. As you are challenged to look at your own leadership, resist the temptation to respond in ways that you wish things were but do not actually reflect your current, up-to-now motivations, attitudes, actions, and beliefs. The truth of the moment may not be pretty. But Jesus said *"the truth will set you free"* (JOHN 8:32) and so it will, when you confront it with honesty and the knowledge that, in Jesus, we have received the ultimate expression of God's unconditional love and forgiveness.

You will find the following icons throughout the text to guide your thinking:

MEMORY VERSE FOR THE WEEK Hiding God's Word in your heart is how you keep your way pure (PS. 119). Take time each week to store this treasure in your heart and mind.

QUOTE OF THE TODAY A wise word to get us started in the right direction.

WHAT GOD'S WORD SAYS We will seek first the kingdom by God by looking to His Word as our source of wisdom and direction. When God's Word speaks specifically of how followers of Jesus are to walk a different path from the world around them in heart, mind, body, and spirit, we will seek not to ask *why*, but rather *how*.

PAUSE AND REFLECT This is an opportunity to consider the proposed concept and to record your reaction to it.

A PRAYER FOR TODAY Following in the habit of Jesus, we will make prayer our first response instead of our last resort. As we invite the Holy Spirit to guide our thoughts, we will take time to read the prayer for the day and offer it up to God as our own.

TODAY'S TOPIC Segments adapted and expanded from *Lead Like Jesus: Lessons from the Greatest Leadership Role Model of All Time*, a book by Ken Blanchard and Phil Hodges on which this study guide is based.

LOOK INSIDE Through the use of a variety of learning tools, questionnaires, and exercises, we will explore our *up-to-now* leadership motivations, thinking, behavior, and habits and how they compare with leading like Jesus.

★ **KEY CONCEPTS** As we explore leading like Jesus, we will discover key principles, concepts, and nonnegotiable mandates that we are not able to accomplish on our own but are called to implement under the guidance of the Holy Spirit.

♀ **A POINT TO PONDER** A thought or idea to keep with us throughout the day.

✈ **NEXT STEPS** *Leading like Jesus* will be a lifetime journey to be traveled in His company step-by-step, moment-by-moment. At the end of each day's lesson, you will be asked to prayerfully consider your Next Steps.

HOW CAN YOU REAP THE GREATEST BENEFITS FROM THIS STUDY?

1. Pray for insight each day as you meet the Lord through this study. Let Him lead you to experience His direction in your life through every learning activity.

2. Experience the focus for each day as you study and apply it to your life. Write down those Aha! ideas that challenge your leadership behaviors and motives. Ask yourself how you can realign your leadership to better reflect Christ's example.

3. Review your progress each week and recognize what God is doing in your life and in the lives of those you lead.

4. Keep a journal in which you will list the action steps and plans associated with your Aha! ideas. Additionally, write down specific ways in which you are putting into practice what you are learning.

5. As your group follows the instructions in the Facilitator's Guide found at **www.LeadLikeJesus. com/FreeStuff**, your knowledge of the principles and their application to everyday life will be multiplied. You cannot learn to lead like Jesus unless you interact with other people. If a small group study isn't possible, invite one or two other people to go through the study with you.

We hope as you learn to trust Jesus as your leadership model, it will make you an active agent for restoring joy to work and family. So whether you're leading in business, nonprofit organizations, your community, your church, or your home, you will make Jesus smile. It is the vision of the Lead Like Jesus ministry (**LeadLikeJesus.com**) that ... that someday everyone, everywhere will be impacted by someone leading like Jesus.

A POINT TO PONDER

Imagine this setting: You, Jesus, and the authors of this *Study Guide* are sitting together conversing about His kind of leadership. Just as the Master Teacher did with His disciples, you will be asked questions, given assignments, and told stories and examples that will help you connect your own experiences with leading like Jesus. So, as you interact with this study guide, invite the Holy Spirit to guide you to new insights and a new perspective on how to put what you learn into practice. Together we will learn to lead like Jesus!

LEAD LIKE JESUS

3506 Professional Circle, Suite B
Augusta, GA 30907
800.383.6890

LeadLikeJesus.com

WE HAVE ALL SEEN LEADERS, IN CORPORATE AMERICA, EXPLOIT PRIVILEGES OF POSITION BRINGING RUIN TO EMPLOYEES AND INVESTORS.

Meanwhile citizens of under-developed countries languish in poverty and hopelessness in a leadership vacuum. At the same time all across the country, the witness and ministry of churches are compromised and stymied by a crisis of integrity in their leaders. In stark contrast to the failures and foibles of 21st Century leadership stands the perfect leadership role model – **Jesus of Nazareth**.

Lead Like Jesus, a 501 (c)(3) organization, co-founded in 1999, by Ken Blanchard, co-author of *The One Minute Manager*, and his longtime friend, Phil Hodges imagines a world in which leaders serve rather than rule, a world in which they give rather than take. We imagine leaders who seek to produce results from service and sacrifice rather than from power and position. We recognize this only happens as leaders adopt Jesus as their leadership role model and grow in His likeness.

We exist to help leaders of all shapes, sizes, ages and aspirations to explore and express the leadership principles Jesus lived. To that end we are both humbled and honored to be entrusted with the stewardship of this vision that "someday, everyone, everywhere will be impacted by someone leading like Jesus."

In MATTHEW 20, Jesus expressed His view of leadership in His *Not So With You* mandate. This principle is a driving force of *Lead Like Jesus*.

For more information on *Lead Like Jesus* or it's programs, services and events, contact: *www.LeadLikeJesus.com*

A LETTER FROM PHYLLIS

Dear Reader,

It is with great excitement that I invite you to dive deep into the Great Leader Study Guides. Jesus knew we would want to be great, so He told us how, with a clear directive that teaches us that greatness comes through service. In fact, servant leadership is the only approach to leadership Jesus ever validates for His followers.

It sounds simple, but serving others does not come easily or naturally. Behavior that demonstrates service comes from a heart that has been transformed by love through a deep connection to the Father. The result is thinking that is others-centered and behavior that seeks to serve. The Great Leader Study Guides were created to help people dig deeper into four areas of growth: The Heart, Head, Hands, and Habits. Our desire is to help you, as a follower of Jesus, reflect Him more and more in every situation, with those you influence.

I pray that out of His glorious riches He may strengthen you with power through His Spirit in your inner being, so that Christ may dwell in your hearts through faith. And I pray that you, being rooted and established in love, may have power, together with all the saints, to grasp how wide and long and high and deep is the love of Christ, and to know this love that surpasses knowledge — that you may be filled to the measure of all the fullness of God.
EPHESIANS 3:16-19

Amen!

Praying for you,

Phyllis H. Hendry
President & CEO
Lead Like Jesus

WEEK ONE
FISHERS OF MEN ... DEVELOPERS OF INDIVIDUALS

 ## MEMORY VERSE FOR THE WEEK

"Come, follow me," Jesus said, "and I will make you fishers of men."
MATTHEW 4:19

The best leaders are rarely star performers. Instead of focusing their energy on developing their skills as a solo performer, they have focused on the skills of a leader: developing others.

"'Come, follow me,' Jesus said, 'and I will make you fishers of men'" (MATTHEW 4:19). Jesus' initial call to His disciples signals His intention for them. Not only will He develop them through a transformative relationship (follow me), the power of that relationship will extend out through them to others.

The next three verses show Jesus calling James and John, both of whom respond immediately. This is followed by a brief three-verse super summary that shows Jesus doing some star performer stuff — all things He could have done before calling the disciples to follow Him. But the performance wasn't for His sake; it was for theirs. It was partly to establish His authority, and it was partly on-the-job training for His new recruits.

The very next verse, MATTHEW 5:1, shows Him getting down to the business of teaching them directly. *Now when he saw the crowds, he went up on a mountainside and sat down. His disciples came to him, and he began to teach them.* His entire ministry revolved around developing His unlikely set of world changers. In developing them, He set the pattern for them to develop others. They did it, and *turned the world upside down* (ACTS 17:6 KJV).

The hands of a leader are all about developing others. Is that your focus?

FISHERS OF MEN ... DEVELOPERS OF INDIVIDUALS
SELF-SERVING LEADER OR SERVANT LEADER?

" QUOTE FOR TODAY

Men are not against you; they are merely for themselves.
GENE FOWLER

📖 WHAT GOD'S WORD SAYS

Your attitude should be the same as that of Christ Jesus: Who, being in very nature God, did not consider equality with God something to be grasped, but made himself nothing, taking the very nature of a servant.
PHILIPPIANS 2:5-7

❚❚ PAUSE AND REFLECT

Have you ever reflected significantly on the times you have been deeply wounded by having your rights violated? Can you recall the righteous indignation you felt — the desire to set things "right"? Can you recall the temptation to allow your righteous indignation to slide in the direction of revenge? If so, congratulations! You pass the humanity test.

Imagine how Jesus must have felt — yielding His rights as Creator and then suffering the indignity of rejection by the very creatures He came to save. But He was prepared.

No leader develops good hands (effective leader behaviors) without doing a lot of heart and head work first. You can't sustain what you do without strong convictions about why you do it. What are your deepest "whys"? Why did you feel wounded? Why did you think you had rights? What rights?

_____

_____

_____

Reread What God's Word Says and reflect on its implications regarding your "rights" and your orientation to servant leadership. How do your behaviors need to adjust to be in alignment with Jesus' example?

_____

_____

_____

🙌 A PRAYER FOR TODAY

Lord, thank You for coming to serve rather than to be served. Thank You for showing us Your love for the Father and Your love for us. Thank You for yielding Your rights and for putting our needs above Your comfort. Thank You for completing Your mission and not stopping short of the ultimate sacrifice. And thank You for Your ability to transform us to reflect You. Help us to desire that above every competing interest. In Jesus' name, Amen!

☀️ TODAY'S TOPIC

Jesus is the lone example of one who could answer the question posed by today's lesson — Self-serving Leader vs. Servant Leader? — in a clear, "either/or," 100 percent positive way. For the rest of us, it's a mixed bag. That's not to say the question is illegitimate; it's a great question. We have to look to the preponderance of evidence — and we have to be brutally honest about our own motives.

We start this study with a reminder that our hands (and to a large degree, our heads) are ruled by our hearts. Most leadership books and seminars focus on the leader's behavior and try to improve leadership style and methods. Emphasis is on the hands of the leader. They attempt to change leadership from the outside. Yet in teaching people to lead like Jesus, we have found that effective leadership starts on the inside; it is a heart issue. We believe if we don't get the heart right, then we simply won't ever become servant leaders like Jesus.

The most persistent barrier to leading like Jesus is a heart motivated by self-interest.

How can we turn this around? We have found three ways that self-serving leaders can see the light and begin to make efforts to serve rather than to be served.

1. A near-death experience when people get in touch with their own mortality: the "Scrooge phenomenon."
2. A spiritual awakening: transformation through a relationship with Jesus.
3. Exposure to a significant model.

We at Lead Like Jesus have the most direct control over the third item in the list. That is why we constantly turn to the Bible for examples that illustrate the unparalleled model of a servant heart that Jesus brought into this world.

 ## LOOK INSIDE

Exposure to Jesus leads to transformation that includes reorienting your heart — turning its values upside down. As painful as it sometimes seems, turning your heart upside down is a necessary first step toward becoming one of *these that have turned the world upside down* (ACTS 17:6 KJV).

How would you describe your progress in resolving the value conflicts that accompany a transformational heart inversion — going from self-serving to others-serving behavior?

Just begun--Complete

1   2   3   4   5

 ## KEY CONCEPT

Our hands (leadership behaviors) are guided by our head and heart, both of which need transformation through ongoing exposure and submission to Jesus.

 ## A POINT TO PONDER

Leading like Jesus is more than a theory; it's about changing the way you lead others ... changing your behavior to be more like Jesus.
KEN BLANCHARD AND PHIL HODGES

NEXT STEPS

What value conflicts are you currently struggling to resolve? One example would be the conflict between protecting your rights and yielding them to God's protection.

_____

_____

_____

_____

Looking at the value conflicts you noted above and the behavior adjustments you noted in the last part of Pause and Reflect, what behavioral guidelines could you develop to train yourself — with God's help — as a servant leader?

_____ _____

_____

_____

_____

THE REWARDS OF SERVANT LEADERSHIP

99 QUOTE FOR TODAY

Above all, servant leaders care about people and want them to flourish and succeed in fulfilling their unique purpose and calling.

KEN BLANCHARD AND PHIL HODGES

WHAT GOD'S WORD SAYS

By faith Moses, when he had grown up, refused to be known as the son of Pharaoh's daughter. He chose to be mistreated along with the people of God rather than to enjoy the pleasures of sin for a short time. He regarded disgrace for the sake of Christ as of greater value than the treasures of Egypt, because he was looking ahead to his reward.

HEBREWS 11:24-26

▌▌ PAUSE AND REFLECT

Imagine being in Moses' situation: on top of the world in a culture so advanced that we – thousands of years later – still marvel at its accomplishments. A future filled with prestige and power beckoned. Suppose you didn't have the benefit of knowing the rest of the story. How would you respond?

_____

_____

_____

Moses made a clear choice to care more about his people than to be served by them. He chose to identify with his slave roots, to walk away from privilege and to embrace disgrace. What would motivate such an outrageous choice? Isn't it interesting that Jesus was at the heart of his motivation – the Christ, who hadn't shown up yet as God/man, but who had shown up as Creator.

Don't think for a moment that your motivation is limited to mere human input. The same God who worked in Moses' heart to provide a prophetic vision and inspirational motivation is at work in your heart. Will you choose to serve or to be served? Why?

_____

_____

_____

🙏 A PRAYER FOR TODAY

Lord, thank You for the example of Moses. Thank You for the way he followed Jesus' pattern of servant leadership. Thank You for providing the vision of Jesus he needed in order to make the right value choice. Thank You for giving him a long-term view, the desire for a greater reward than the riches and sophistication of Egypt. Help me to have that same long-term view. Please transform my heart. In Jesus' name, Amen!

☼ TODAY'S TOPIC

Until the law of cause and effect is suspended, every choice has its reward. Some rewards turn out to be consequences — this usually happens when we don't have enough discernment to realize that a given choice promises a reward it can't deliver. Think of the last time you chose not to tell the whole truth because you didn't want to sacrifice your image. The consequence was that you sacrificed it anyway — at least in your own eyes. Or how about the times you didn't step up to leadership in your family because your career seemed to deliver more significance?

On the other hand, some choices deliver rewards that far exceed what they promise. Such choices typically involve daily investments, small sacrifices that seem unexciting and relatively insignificant: building a marriage relationship, parenting, mentoring, nurturing a friendship, helping someone in need.

God has a habit of under-promising and over-delivering. When He delivers, we are often amazed and baffled. Consider the example of a story Jesus told. *Then the King will say to those on his right, 'Come, you who are blessed by my Father; take your inheritance, the kingdom prepared for you since the creation of the world'* (MATTHEW 25:34). The inheritors didn't understand. Their minds jammed over one question: What have we done to deserve this?

God delights in saying "Surprise!" Listen to how He answered their question: *I tell you the truth, whatever you did for one of the least of these brothers of mine, you did for me* (MATTHEW 25:40).

Could Jesus have made the rewards of servant leadership any clearer? He lived the message, taught it, died to prove it, and rose again to ensure it. Look how the writer of Hebrews describes Jesus making His choice with the reward in mind: Jesus *... for the joy set before him endured the cross ...* (HEBREWS 12:2).

 **LOOK INSIDE**

Do you have a subconscious bias that believes self-serving leadership offers the best rewards? Before quickly saying "no," consider the fact that we are all born with that bias. It is not only our natural state but also reinforced by our culture.

Leaders rank high in competitiveness, and success is often equated with winning, finishing first. In spite of efforts to teach otherwise, there is a haunting cynicism whispering in our ear: it insists that good guys finish last.

Could you be subconsciously discounting the value of God's "Surprise!"?

 KEY CONCEPT

Servant leadership involves self-sacrifice in the sense that it is others-oriented, but there is no sacrifice of reward. The rewards come in stages — small and subtle at first but appreciating over time and exploding into eternal joy.

 A POINT TO PONDER

The next time you wonder whether servant leadership is worth the effort, remember this: God doesn't expect you to serve for nothing. In fact, He has made it absolutely impossible.

 NEXT STEPS

What kind of reward do you anticipate from your leadership choices?

_____

_____

_____

Have you carefully examined whose reward you're trusting? God under-promises and over-delivers; Satan, the deceiver, does just the opposite. While God calls us to commitment before reward, Satan lures us with a reward first — a reward that quickly morphs into guilt and condemnation.

You are constantly training your ear to tune in to one voice in a sea of conflicting of voices. Whose voice are you straining to identify and follow? What steps will you take to examine the rewards you anticipate? How will you determine their source and reliability?

_____

_____

_____

_____

FISHERS OF MEN ... DEVELOPERS OF INDIVIDUALS

THE SERVANT LEADER AS A PERFORMANCE COACH

QUOTE FOR TODAY

This is the duty of the servant leader — the ongoing investment of the leader's life into the lives of those who follow.

KEN BLANCHARD AND PHIL HODGES

WHAT GOD'S WORD SAYS

When Jesus had called the Twelve together, he gave them power and authority ... and he sent them out to preach the kingdom of God and to heal the sick. He told them ... So they set out .... When the apostles returned, they reported to Jesus what they had done. Then he took them with him and they withdrew by themselves to a town called Bethsaida.

LUKE 9:1-6, 10

PAUSE AND REFLECT

The chapters preceding Luke 9 in What God's Word Says above are filled with accounts of Jesus healing people. Chapter 7 tells of Jesus raising a man from the dead. *People were all filled with awe and praised God ... This news about Jesus spread throughout Judea and the surrounding country* (LUKE 7:16-17).

Imagine you had this kind of star performance power. Would you want to waste your time coaching a supporting cast? How do you explain Jesus' continuing time commitment to His disciples?

_____

_____

_____

A PRAYER FOR TODAY

Lord, You know the self-centeredness of my heart — the battle I fight daily to focus on the needs of others. Please help me to love with Jesus' kind of love and to invest in those who follow me. Help me to recognize that relationships are more than just a means to an end. In Jesus' name, Amen!

☀ TODAY'S TOPIC

Jesus followed His promise to make His recruits fishers of men by spending significant time with them in every phase of the training process. In Luke 9, we see Him planning with them, instructing, empowering, and debriefing them.

What appears as a brief summary would have taken hours — probably days of preparation. The point? This use of time was clearly worth it to Jesus; it was a pattern He frequently repeated during His brief three years of public ministry.

There are three parts to becoming a performance coach: performance planning, day-to-day coaching, and performance evaluation. Performance planning is all about providing direction and setting goals. Day-to-day coaching involves helping people win — accomplish their goals — by observing their performance, praising progress, and redirecting efforts that are off base. That leads to the third part of performance coaching; performance evaluation. That requires sitting down with people and evaluating their performance over time.

Performance planning is giving people the final exam ahead of time — supplying them with what they need to excel, to accomplish the right priorities. Jesus planned His recruits' strategy carefully before sending them out. Then He gave them the power and authority they needed to succeed in their mission. We can do the same for those whom we lead. Although we cannot empower to the same degree Jesus did, we can and must give appropriate authority whenever we delegate. Effective leaders value the delegation process as being much more than a way to shed busy work. Ideally, it is what Jesus elevated it to: a means of developing and motivating His recruits. Although they were unremarkable men, He determined to make them into world changers.

 ## LOOK INSIDE

How much time do you allocate specifically to performance coaching?

Hours per week	1	3	5	10	15	?
Percentage of time	2%	6%	10%	20%	30%	?

What do you think would be ideal in your circumstances?

_____

_____

_____

 KEY CONCEPT

A key activity of an effective servant leader is to act as a performance coach.

 A POINT TO PONDER

You feed maturity every time you choose to allow your concern for others to outweigh your concern for yourself.
CHIP BROGDEN

NEXT STEPS

If there is not clear communication of what a good job will look like when it is accomplished somebody will end up frustrated — either the leader or the follower or both. Have you prepared "final exams" for those you coach? Determine and record these for each.

_____

_____

_____

_____

_____

PERFORMANCE COACH — ROUND TWO

99 QUOTE FOR TODAY

Coaching is the most important servant leadership element in helping people to accomplish their goals.

KEN BLANCHARD AND PHIL HODGES

WHAT GOD'S WORD SAYS

After this the Lord appointed seventy-two others and sent them two by two ... He told them, "Ask ... Go ... Do not ... When you enter a house, first say ... Stay ... Do not ... When you enter a town ... eat ... Heal ... tell them ... But when you enter ... He who listens to you listens to me; he who rejects you rejects me; but he who rejects me rejects him who sent me." The seventy-two returned with joy and said, "Lord, even the demons submit to us in your name."

Then he turned to his disciples and said privately, "Blessed are the eyes that see what you see. For I tell you that many prophets and kings wanted to see what you see but did not see it, and to hear what you hear but did not hear it."

LUKE 10:1-17, 23-24

❚❚ PAUSE AND REFLECT

Read the entire text of LUKE 10:1-24 abbreviated in What God's Word Says to see how detailed and specific Jesus' instructions were. Think back to a time when you were on either side of a failure in communication on what was expected and what was delivered. Recall the frustration and wasted energy that could have been avoided by testing for understanding

_____

_____

_____

🙏 A PRAYER FOR TODAY

Lord, thank You for the explicit direction Jesus provided — in both what He said and what He did. And thank You for giving me a Coach in the person of Your Spirit, who resides in me and helps me know how to apply what Jesus said. I want to be effective as a leader for those whom You place in my care. Please help me to coach like Jesus did. In Jesus' name, Amen!

 **TODAY'S TOPIC**

We talk (in The Head of a Great Leader) about the normal leadership pyramid and the leader's role to determine direction from the top. Then we show the pyramid inverting in implementation; the hierarchy turning upside down so that the leader is serving those on the front lines. This begins with day-to-day coaching ... teaching people the right answers.

When this doesn't happen, the traditional hierarchy is kept in place and all of the energy of the organization is moving away from the customers and up the hierarchy. Now, pleasing the boss becomes the goal, because he or she is the key to a good performance review. This is typical of an organization where day-to-day coaching is the least-used component of the three-part management system (performance planning, day-to-day coaching, and performance evaluation).

Don't give in to the pattern of giving people the benefit of a little planning, a little coaching, and a lot of performance review. It may be common, but it doesn't produce the results you want. Coaching your people to perform at the top of their capacity is just good sense.

Servant leaders aren't threatened by people around them who perform well. They want people to win. When people win, the family or organization wins.

Notice two additional things in the Luke passage above.

1. Jesus underscores His followers' significance when He says, *"He who listens to you listens to me; he who rejects you rejects me; but he who rejects me rejects him who sent me."*

2. Jesus underscores His followers' privilege when He says, *"Blessed are the eyes that see what you see. For I tell you that many prophets and kings wanted to see what you see but did not see it, and to hear what you hear but did not hear it."*

Although it isn't appropriate for you to use Jesus' words, the principle still applies. Part of your coaching is enhancing your followers' sense of both significance and privilege: significance, as in potential influence, and privilege, as in rare opportunity. This is a motivating combination.

 LOOK INSIDE

At the very center of Luke 10 is a startling statement: At that time Jesus, full of joy through the Holy Spirit, said, *'I praise you, Father, Lord of heaven and earth, because you have hidden these things from the wise and learned, and revealed them to little children. Yes, Father, for this was your good pleasure'* (LUKE 10:21).

Could your followers report you being full of joy and praising God for His plan? When is the last time you took obvious delight in how God was at work in your life and the lives of your followers?

_____

_____

_____

_____

 ## KEY CONCEPT

Performance coaching multiplies your influence and reinforces your culture en route to achieving your vision.

 ## A POINT TO PONDER

We help people get A's the same way Jesus did as He developed His disciples from untrained novices to master teacher disciples.

 ## NEXT STEPS

Think of how God is at work in you and your people. At what can you rejoice? Think of how you can communicate this to underscore your followers' significance and privilege.

_____

_____

_____

_____

_____

_____

_____

FISHERS OF MEN ... DEVELOPERS OF INDIVIDUALS
FROM CALL TO COMMISSION

99 QUOTE FOR TODAY

It is by attempting to reach the top at a single leap that so much misery is caused in the world.

WILLIAM COBBETT

WHAT GOD'S WORD SAYS

And the things you have heard me say in the presence of many witnesses entrust to reliable men who will also be qualified to teach others.

2 TIMOTHY 2:2

▌▌ PAUSE AND REFLECT

Consider the Quote of the Day above along with these: "It is a mistake to look too far ahead. Only one link in the chain of destiny can be handled at a time" — SIR WINSTON CHURCHILL. "One thing at a time, all things in succession. That which grows slowly endures" — J.G. HUBBARD.

How does Paul's directive from **2 TIMOTHY 2:2** in What God's Word Says assume the need for taking a long view? How do you overcome our current culture's emphasis on the short view?

_____

_____

_____

_____

🙏 A PRAYER FOR TODAY

Lord, thank You for calling me out of a life of bondage, a life marked primarily by striving for self-satisfaction. And thank You for commissioning me to a vision (**Go and make disciples ...**) greater than I can ever fulfill. Help me to learn the wisdom of small, consistent investments in the lives of others. In Jesus' name, Amen

TODAY'S TOPIC

When Jesus first called the disciples from their ordinary occupations to become "fishers of men," each brought life experiences and skills to this new task but no practical knowledge of how to fulfill this new role. After spending three years under the leadership of Jesus, the disciples were transformed from untrained novices to fully equipped, inspired and spiritually grounded leaders able to fulfill the Great Commission to go to all nations with the good news.

We believe the experience Jesus had as a learner, under instruction as a carpenter, provided Him with a practical model for growing and developing people that He was able to use to guide the learning experience of His disciples from call to commission.

Having presumably been guided through four normal stages of learning a new task — from novice (someone just starting out) to apprentice (someone in training) to journeyman (someone capable of working independently) and finally master/teacher (someone highly skilled and able to teach others) — of the carpenter craft. Jesus brought to His season of leadership a clear understanding of the journey from dependence to independence.

 ## LOOK INSIDE

Asking yourself, "What would Jesus do?" before you act as a leader is a good practice, but it only raises the question. How you answer the question is crucial. To what degree is your answer informed by the answer to this question: What did Jesus do?

 ## KEY CONCEPT

To progress from being a novice to becoming a master in any role or skill, learners need someone to guide them along the way and to give them what they need to advance through the learning process.

A POINT TO PONDER

Developing people is a process; the accumulation of many incremental advances takes time.

Consider Elihu Burrit's observation from his own life. "All that I have accomplished ... has been by that plodding, patient, persevering process of accretion which builds the ant heap particle by particle, thought by thought, fact by fact."

Your calling as a leader means giving the necessary time to the process.

✈ NEXT STEPS

Mere supposition about what Jesus would do — without examining what He did do — sometimes lends religious fervor to mistaken conclusions. This is why we spend so much time examining exactly what He said, what He did, and what He said about why He did what He did. We want to get it right; we want to be *qualified to teach others* as Paul urged.

How can you improve your understanding of what Jesus **did** so that you can improve your understanding of what He **would** do?

CONGRATULATIONS!

Having reached the end of Week 1, you are about to embark on one of the most valuable parts of this study. Your answers to two simple application questions will open the door to growth as a leader. It's not just the theory you know but how you apply and practice it that helps you become someone who leads like Jesus.

In light of what you have learned this week:

How can you be different in your approach as a leader? As a follower?

_____

_____

_____

_____

What can you do right now — or within a week — to begin demonstrating this difference so that others can see it?

_____

_____

_____

_____

WEEK TWO
ONE SIZE DOES NOT FIT ALL

 MEMORY VERSE FOR THE WEEK

And Jesus grew in wisdom and stature, and in favor with God and men.
LUKE 2:52

As a performance coach, you quickly realize that what is effective with one person may not work with another. There are many reasons for this, including age, gender, maturity, temperament, processing preferences, the nature of your relationship, etc. If you are a good learner, the more experience you have with a diversity of people, the more you know about these differences and adjust for them.

But there is another kind of difference that is crucial — whether in the workplace or at home. When you attempt to coach a person's performance, you need to understand the nature of their present ability level. This is obvious in the sense that it drives the information they need, but there is a less obvious component, which is no less important.

The process of learning a new task advances sequentially through four stages: from *novice* (someone just starting out) to *apprentice* (someone in training) to *journeyman* (someone capable of working independently) and finally *master/teacher* (someone highly skilled and able to teach others). Each stage has different information needs but different presentation needs. For maximum effectiveness, your focus and the style of your presentation must accommodate the learning stage of the person you're coaching.

Once you understand this, your coaching becomes more efficient and more effective. An important caution: although people are in only one stage at a time with a given skill or role, they are in multiple learning stages at any given time — with regard to multiple skills or roles.

It is easier to identify a person's learning stage when you dissect the skill or role under consideration from the rest of the person's skills and roles. A surgeon, for instance, may be a master/teacher in certain areas of medicine but be a novice in counseling patients. The way you coach him in surgery would be considerably different from the way you would coach him in interpersonal communication.

This week's study focuses on the unique needs of each learning stage. The experience Jesus had as a learner, under instruction as a carpenter, provided Him with the knowledge He used to coach His recruits through the entire learning-stage spectrum.

ONE SIZE DOES NOT FIT ALL
THE NEEDS OF A NOVICE

99 QUOTE FOR TODAY

The highest reward for a man's work is not what he gets for it but what he becomes by it.
JOHN RUSKIN

WHAT GOD'S WORD SAYS

On hearing this, Jesus said, "It is not the healthy who need a doctor, but the sick. But go and learn what this means: 'I desire mercy, not sacrifice.' For I have not come to call the righteous, but sinners."
MATTHEW 9:12-14

❚❚ PAUSE AND REFLECT

Most novices are soon confronted by a brutal truth: what looked so easy when done by the master seems impossible in early attempts. Can you remember how discouraging it was? How it made you want to jump to another conclusion: that this clearly wasn't for you?

Sometimes you probably ran the other way, but sometimes you decided to keep trying. The difference may have been a caring person — someone who was willing to encourage you and patiently walk you through the basics. You didn't need the subtle twist that could squeeze another one percent out of your performance; you needed simple information that would seem painfully obvious to anyone with any experience.

Recall a difficult learning memory from your own past and allow it to inform your style with novices.

_____

_____

_____

_____

_____

🙏 A PRAYER FOR TODAY

Lord, thank You for giving me people I can encourage and teach in the same way I have received effective help. Even though I don't spend a lot of time with people that I think of as novices, I realize that they are novices in some areas. Help me to adjust accordingly when I am helping them at the novice level. In Jesus' name, Amen!

☀ TODAY'S TOPIC

Novices enter the learning process through an orientation phase. They are just starting out to perform a particular task or to accomplish an assigned goal. They need to know what, when, where, why, and how to do something, but they can't absorb it all at once.

Effective coaching requires understanding the basic sequence — what information has to precede other information so that excess information doesn't get in the way. An overwhelmed student is more likely to quit than to develop competence.

Jesus' statement in today's What God's Word Says comes on the heels of recruiting Matthew — a tax collector. Immediately confronted by Pharisees over His choice of companions, Jesus seizes a teaching moment. Not only is He teaching a new recruit, He is also addressing a highly educated group who should already know the message. Unfortunately, they are clearly novices in the behavior Jesus wants to teach.

Go and learn what this means, He says, and then He quotes the prophet Hosea: *I desire mercy, not sacrifice* (HOSEA 6:6). He doesn't give these novices advanced theology; He shows them basics. He had come to demonstrate the loving character of God that their hardened hearts had long since abandoned.

First, He showed it through His behavior — eating with tax collectors and sinners. Then He used the simple medical analogy that even a child could understand. Finally, He follows with a clear statement of His purpose.

Someone could argue that Jesus' approach wasn't effective with these novices, but evidence for such an argument would be limited to the Pharisees — the perceived experts who did not possess a learner's heart. They would have refused any instruction that threatened their self-righteous monopoly.

True novices, those who are striving to learn something new, responded — and continue to respond — very well. Do you remember Jesus' spontaneous prayer of praise mentioned in last week's study?

I praise you, Father, Lord of heaven and earth, because you have hidden these things from the wise and learned, and revealed them to little children (LUKE 10:21). God is very conscious of the needs of novices, and Jesus took great care not only to include them but to make them the center of His focus.

 **LOOK INSIDE**

Although you may be a master/teacher in some roles, in what roles might you be a novice? One of the benefits of learning new skills is that it keeps you in touch with the coaching needs of a novice. Develop a conscious awareness of any obstacles or insecurities you experience; they can increase your effectiveness as a coach.

_____

_____

_____

_____

 KEY CONCEPT

Leading like Jesus with novices includes providing basic information and being committed to their development.

A POINT TO PONDER

Success is going from failure to failure without loss of enthusiasm.
SIR WINSTON CHURCHILL

Since novices are bound to experience a high frequency of failure, loss of enthusiasm becomes a high risk. They need patience, bolstered by the acknowledgement that what looks easy is not easy.

Coaches also need patience, realizing that what seems so easy to them was not always easy. Understanding the novice's frustration and potential loss of enthusiasm is a key to providing necessary emotional support, which is sometimes as crucial as the basic information. This is why we say novices need basic information **and** someone committed to their development.

✈ NEXT STEPS

As you think of the people you are leading and coaching, make a list of those who are in the novice category. Don't overlook experienced people who are novices in a particular role. Although a seasoned professional learning a new skill may not have identical needs to a young novice, it might surprise you how similar the needs are.

After compiling your list, go name by name and think of a coaching contribution or an adjustment you can make that might speed their progress.

Name	Contribution/Adjustment

ONE SIZE DOES NOT FIT ALL
THE NEEDS OF AN APPRENTICE

99 QUOTE FOR TODAY

Only he who does nothing makes no mistakes.
FRENCH PROVERB

WHAT GOD'S WORD SAYS

I pray that out of his glorious riches he may strengthen you with power through his Spirit in your inner being, so that Christ may dwell in your hearts through faith.
EPHESIANS 3:16-17

❚❚ PAUSE AND REFLECT

Meditate for a few moments on the prayer in What God's Word Says that Paul prayed for the apprentice believers in Ephesus. He was very aware of their deepest need, and he labored for them in prayer regarding it.

- Do you have anyone praying for you like that?

- Have you asked anyone to pray earnestly for you regarding something more substantial than a health or employment need — something that relates to the ongoing need of your inner being?

- Are you praying that way for those you lead and coach?

🙏 A PRAYER FOR TODAY

Lord, thank You for placing Your Spirit in me to help me do what I can't do in my own strength. Help me to see through the clutter of the urgent and to recognize the deeper needs in myself and in those I serve. Help me to develop the discipline of striving in prayer — as Paul and Jesus frequently did. In Jesus' name, Amen!

☀ TODAY'S TOPIC

Apprentices are people in training who have not yet mastered all the information and skills they need to work alone. They need to be assured that they are doing the right thing in the right way and to be corrected when they don't quite "have it." They also need someone to put their progress in the right perspective so they don't become overconfident with early success or discouraged with initial failure.

Accurate feedback is valuable for anyone — from the novice to the master/teacher — because it enables us to adjust and improve our performance.

The length of time it takes an apprentice to transition to a journeyman is dependent on many factors, but one of the most important is the timeliness and quality of feedback received. When there is no clear connection between cause and effect, the effect is likely to be attributed to the wrong cause — including dumb luck. Apprentices need help connecting the dots between their actions and their results. Without that help, they waste time reproducing their effort without adjustments or by making irrelevant adjustments.

MATTHEW 17:14-21 shows the apprentice disciples asking Jesus for feedback after failing to drive out a demon — one of the tasks He had assigned them earlier. Imagine what their conversation with each other might have sounded like before getting Jesus' answer. They probably wondered whether they had said exactly the right words in the right order or whether they had touched the boy the right way or whether they should have held hands while they prayed or ... But Jesus nailed it. In this case, He revealed a need in their inner being — a need for greater faith.

We all have that same need. It is a spiritual force, a strengthening *with power through his Spirit.* Your leadership is much more than a collection of skills and techniques. It's more than applied knowledge. It is empowerment by the Spirit to do what is impossible by human effort: to love God with all your heart and to love your neighbor as yourself. Anyone who gets anywhere near that standard is a leader of rare distinction.

💼 LOOK INSIDE

Think of a time when you were an apprentice in the development of a difficult skill. Since people vary considerably in natural giftedness, your most difficult tasks may have been easy for others — and vice versa. Can you recall a task or component that was especially difficult for you, one that you spent excessive time to master?

_____

_____

_____

_____

Repeated failures in training, provided the apprentice does not give up, often result in a superior level of mastery. Identifying an example in your own experience can help you coach an apprentice through a challenge that feels impossible.

_____

_____

_____

 KEY CONCEPT

> Leading like Jesus with apprentices includes assuring them that they are doing the right thing in the right way and correcting when they don't quite "have it."

 A POINT TO PONDER

> Delayed feedback, like delayed consequences for a child, loses a lot of effectiveness.

NEXT STEPS

If you are not already in a committed prayer relationship with someone who "has your back" on a regular basis, with whom will you seek to begin one?

_____

_____

_____

_____

How can you improve the timeliness and quality of the feedback you give?

_____

_____

_____

_____

How can you pray for the deeper needs of your apprentices?

_____

_____

_____

_____

WEEK 2

DAY 3

ONE SIZE DOES NOT FIT ALL
THE NEEDS OF A JOURNEYMAN

QUOTE FOR TODAY

Who needs encouragement? Anyone who is breathing.
TRUETT CATHY

WHAT GOD'S WORD SAYS

I pray that you, being rooted and established in love, may have power, together with all the saints, to grasp how wide and long and high and deep is the love of Christ, and to know this love that surpasses knowledge.
EPHESIANS 3:17-19

PAUSE AND REFLECT

The prayer in today's What God's Word Says is a continuation of Paul's prayer from yesterday. You can see a clear progression from yesterday's apprentice stage to today's journeyman stage. How would you describe your *power to grasp* the magnitude of *Christ's love* in a way that *surpasses knowledge?*

_____

_____

_____

_____

A PRAYER FOR TODAY

Lord, thank You for the depth of love and commitment You have for me. Thank You for allowing me to experience it and grow in my awareness of it even though it is beyond comprehension. Help me to remember that *what is seen is temporary, but what is unseen is eternal.* I want to live in the power of Your Spirit. In Jesus' name, Amen!

☼ TODAY'S TOPIC

The journeyman's primary needs move beyond learning and practicing new skills. But the fact that they now have enough competence to work on their own most of the time doesn't mean they can be left alone. They may periodically become cautious, lose confidence, or have a diminished sense of enthusiasm for the job due to a variety of reasons.

Journeymen can lose their skills and ability to perform and become disillusioned critics and skeptics who poison the attitude of those who work around them. Leaders who ignore the needs of journeymen for appreciation, encouragement, and inspiration do so at their own peril.

Appreciation, encouragement, and inspiration are not skill-based needs; they are needs that go much deeper. Our inability to fully comprehend them tempts us to think of them as soft, intangible, and even unreal. But they are certainly not unreal to our emotions, and no leader denies the power of emotions — either to motivate or de-motivate.

When Paul prayed that the Ephesians would *grasp ... the love of Christ ... that surpasses knowledge*, he was acknowledging a deeper knowing than our minds can comprehend. Appreciation, encouragement, and inspiration are like that; whether you know how they work or not, you can trust that they do work and that journeymen need them.

Peter, as a journeyman disciple, walked on the water toward Jesus just fine. For awhile. But when he saw the wind, he was afraid and, beginning to sink, cried out, *'Lord, save me!' Immediately Jesus reached out his hand and caught him. 'You of little faith,' he said, 'why did you doubt?'* (MATTHEW 14:30-31).

Journeymen will sometimes doubt their ability to apply their skills to new and unusual circumstances. They may take their eye off the ball and focus on the wind. When they do, they are likely to lose their footing and need rescue. Jesus understood this and provided the hand that was needed.

Your hands as a leader are sometimes needed to rescue; they are always needed to provide appreciation, encouragement, and inspiration.

LOOK INSIDE

Peter was no stranger to failure. He was willing to plunge into — and bungle — all kinds of situations. Many leaders may have seen the loose cannon he was and sent him packing. But Jesus saw something more. He saw someone on a journey — through fits and starts — toward becoming a master/teacher, a leader, one of those who *turned the world upside down* (ACTS 17:6 KJV).

What do you see in others? What are you looking for? Part of that answer comes from what you see in yourself and your humble acknowledgement of the role other leaders in your life have played in rescuing you and providing appreciation, encouragement, and inspiration when you failed.

_____

_____

_____

_____

★ KEY CONCEPT

Leading like Jesus with journeymen includes providing rescue, appreciation, encouragement, and inspiration.

💡 A POINT TO PONDER

Peter's consistent pattern of impetuous failures would have tested the continuing commitment of any leader. Jesus' commitment never wavered.

This is not to suggest that employees should never be demoted or dismissed. Nor is it to suggest that you should have the perfect insight of Jesus and the empowering ability of the Holy Spirit to develop a floundering failure into a world changer. It does suggest, however, an uncommon commitment to developing people through coaching and, as Paul demonstrates with the Ephesians, praying for their *inner being.*

✈ NEXT STEPS

Look at the journeymen you are leading. Do you know them well enough to discern hidden needs? What adjustments can you make in your dealings with them to get to know them better — both inside and out?

_____

_____

_____

_____

What steps can you take to remind yourself to pray for them consistently, especially regarding the hidden needs they have?

_____

_____

_____

_____

ONE SIZE DOES NOT FIT ALL
THE NEEDS OF A MASTER/TEACHER

99 QUOTE FOR TODAY

I long to accomplish a great and noble task, but it is my chief duty to accomplish small tasks as if they were great and noble.

HELEN KELLER

WHAT GOD'S WORD SAYS

... that you may be filled to the measure of all the fullness of God.
EPHESIANS 3:19

As you sent me into the world, I have sent them into the world ... I have given them the glory that you gave me, that they may be one as we are one: I in them and you in me.
JOHN 17:18, 22-23

▌▌ PAUSE AND REFLECT

Over the last few days, we've seen Paul's prayer for the Ephesians unfold. It is prophetic and full of faith as he pictures them transitioning from apprentices to journeymen to the full maturity of master/teachers. Imagine being *filled to the measure of all the fullness of God*!

Jesus' prayer for His disciples pays them the ultimate compliment when He tells the Father that He is in them and has sent them into the world. This extends also to us: *My prayer is not for them alone. I pray also for those who will believe in me through their message, that all of them may be one, Father, just as you are in me and I am in you* (JOHN 17:20-21).

Imagine the Creator entrusting His mission to a motley group of commoners He called to become fishers of men! Leading them through a three-year journey from novices to master/teachers who *turned the world upside down* is certainly the model we want to emulate.

_____

_____

_____

_____

🙏 A PRAYER FOR TODAY

O Lord, You are my God; I will exalt You and praise Your name, for in perfect faithfulness You have done marvelous things, things planned long ago. Thank You, Lord, for Your promise to complete what You began in us. Please increase our faith. Help us to stop relying on our limited human abilities. Help us to stop aiming at targets so far below Your eternal plans for us. May we fix our eyes on You and be filled with faith in Your strength. In Jesus' name, Amen!

☀ TODAY'S TOPIC

Master/teachers are people with fully developed skills, confidence, and motivation to produce excellent results as individual performers, as well as the wisdom and insight to teach others. They need to be given the opportunity and challenge to pass on what they know to the next generation of learners — and they need your blessing.

So what are the needs of a master/teacher?

_____

_____

_____

_____

Opportunity: You give them opportunity when, like Jesus, you entrust them with responsibility and the appropriate authority to fulfill it.

Challenge: You challenge them when you communicate the vision of a great vision — a vision that requires the imagination of faith.

Blessing: You bless them when you affirm your full support and your confidence in their ability to fulfill the vision.

Jesus modeled all of these in His parting words. *All power is given unto me in heaven and in earth. Go ye therefore, and teach all nations, baptizing them in the name of the Father, and of the Son, and of the Holy Ghost: Teaching them to observe all things whatsoever I have commanded you: and, lo, I am with you always, even unto the end of the world* (MATTHEW 28:18-20).

LOOK INSIDE

As you contemplate the prayers of Paul and Jesus, do they reflect your desire for those you lead? To what extent are you committed to helping the master/teachers you lead fulfill the vision God has for them?

_____

_____

_____

KEY CONCEPT

Leading like Jesus with master/teachers includes providing opportunity, challenge and blessing.

A POINT TO PONDER

To lead like Jesus is to have the attitude of a servant. **Let this mind be in you, which was also in Christ Jesus: Who, being in the form of God, thought it not robbery to be equal with God: But made himself of no reputation, and took upon him the form of a servant** (PHILIPPIANS 2:5-7).

Servant leadership doesn't just catch and keep people. Neither is it a simple catch and release exercise. Servant leadership at its best captures imagination, improves performance, and then releases to fulfill. It says: These are not my people; they are God's people. He has given me the responsibility of serving them in a way that is beneficial to the Kingdom, to themselves, and to me. When I lead this way, there are no losers.

NEXT STEPS

What should change in your training to make you successful at capturing peoples' imagination, improving their performance, and releasing them to fulfill the vision?

_____

_____

_____

_____

LEADER/FOLLOWER PARTNERSHIP

99 QUOTE FOR TODAY

People seldom improve when they have no other model than themselves to copy.
OLIVER GOLDSMITH

WHAT GOD'S WORD SAYS

"Come, follow me," Jesus said, "and I will make you fishers of men."
MATTHEW 4:19

I have made you known to them, and will continue to make you known in order that the love you have for me may be in them and that I myself may be in them.
JOHN 17:26

▌▌ PAUSE AND REFLECT

The verses in today's What God's Word Says are both statements made by Jesus, bookends revealing His commitment and its completion. The first statement pictures the commitment He offers His recruits if they choose to follow Him — a strong, confident commitment. It will require their submission and active participation, but there is no hint of uncertainty.

The second statement comes near the end of His direct training time with them as He is declaring that part of His mission accomplished and commending them to the Father. His partnership with them in making them *fishers of men* has been successful because He discerned what they needed and provided it at the appropriate time.

Who has been a partner with you in your development? Although no one could measure up to Jesus' level of commitment, you can probably name several people who have provided some of your needs at various learning stages.

_____

_____

_____

_____

🙏 A PRAYER FOR TODAY

Lord, thank You for Your commitment to me and for providing people who have filled vital roles in my development. Please bring into my life the people for whom You want me to play a similar role. Help me view the people I lead in the same way You viewed the disciples — with love, commitment, and positive expectation. In Jesus' name, Amen!

☀ TODAY'S TOPIC

Learners are growers, on the move toward higher levels of development and responsibility. As they move from novice toward master/teacher, they need a leadership partner who can give them direction and support. A successful learner-development process is a mutual commitment.

Effective leadership partners discern what stage learners are in and when they are approaching the next stage. They understand that no one is totally a novice, apprentice, journeyman, or master/teacher in all roles or skills. At any one time in our work life or in one of our life role relationships, we could be at all four learning stages: a novice on a new computer program, an apprentice on budgeting, a journeyman on people development, and a master at planning.

A learner with multiple roles or skills under development may have a leadership partner involved with several of them. The leadership partner would deal with the same learner in different ways depending on which role or skill was being addressed. Imagine a child who is great at reading but struggles with math. Using the same teaching style for both of these subjects with this child would be a disaster.

This chart shows the four learning stages and the primary needs of each.

LEARNING STAGES			
Novice (Someone just starting out)	Apprentice (someone in training)	Journeyman (someone able to work independently)	Master (someone able to teach others)
LEADERSHIP PARTNER PROVIDES			
Instructing Basic information: What, How, Where, When, Why	Coaching Instruction, Practice and Evaluation	Mentoring Assignment and Encouragement	Commissioning Affirmation and Autonomy

LOOK INSIDE

How aware are you of the learning stages of the people you are coaching? Is it possible that you could be providing Person A with what Person B needs? Or providing Person A with what he or she needs in a different area of development?

Think of your own needs in your current learning stages and consider what is most helpful to you in each.

_____

_____

_____

_____

KEY CONCEPT

A successful learner-development process is a mutual commitment between a leader and learner in which they jointly draw conclusions and agree on:

1. Goals and objectives for the follower

2. The learning stage of the follower for each goal

3. What the follower needs at each stage for each goal and how the leader will provide it

4. When the follower is shifting to a new learning stage and what that means to their relationship

A POINT TO PONDER

The most important single influence in the life of a person is another person ... who is worthy of emulation.
PAUL D. SHAFER

Most importantly, this is Jesus. Secondarily, it is Jesus "with skin on" — someone walking with you in real time who can assist your leadership development.

✈ NEXT STEPS

Consider the people you are responsible for coaching or who look to you for coaching. Determine what stage they are in for any given role or skill with which you are assisting them.

_____

_____

_____

How will you adjust your coaching to be as effective as possible because of what you are discovering about learning stages?

_____

_____

_____

CONGRATULATIONS!

Week 2 has shown you the importance of coaching individuals in light of their learning stage. Your answers to our two application questions will help you put your knowledge into practice. Don't forget that it's not just the theory you know but how you apply and practice it that helps you become someone who leads like Jesus.

In light of what you have learned this week: How can you be different in your approach as a leader? As a follower?

_____

_____

_____

What can you do right now — or within a week — to begin demonstrating this difference so that others can see it?

_____

_____

_____

WEEK THREE
CLASSIC CLASHES BETWEEN LEADERS AND FOLLOWERS

 ## MEMORY VERSE FOR THE WEEK

Finally, all of you, live in harmony with one another; be sympathetic, love as brothers, be compassionate and humble.
1 PETER 3:8

Ask any leader; clashes are inevitable.

Ask enough leaders and you will quickly compile a long list of causes, everything from differences of opinion or incompetence on the benign end to jealousy and rebellion on the other.

We believe that most clashes are emotional collisions involving some combination of pride and fear. Understanding root causes is a valuable step in resolving clashes. This week's study exposes the four most common combinations of pride and fear in leader-follower relationships. Explore these — not only to discover root causes in others but also to recognize them in yourself.

Clashes may be inevitable, but they do not have to last. You, as the leader, have the primary responsibility to make the first move toward resolution.

Servant leadership is characterized by a focus that shifts from egocentric to others-centric. *For we do not preach ourselves, but Jesus Christ as Lord, and ourselves as your servants for Jesus' sake* (2 CORINTHIANS 4:5).

We strive to develop the attitude of Jesus, *who for the joy that was set before him endured the cross* (HEBREWS 12:2). This requires constantly reminding ourselves — because it is contrary to our fallen human nature — that love-motivated sacrifices have a long-term payoff beyond anything we give up. *For our light and momentary troubles are achieving for us an eternal glory that far outweighs them all* (2 CORINTHIANS 4: 17).

Clashes come and clashes go; and the sooner they go, the better. Relationships have eternal value.

CLASSIC CLASHES BETWEEN LEADERS AND FOLLOWERS
EGO IN LEADER-FOLLOWER RELATIONSHIPS

99 QUOTE FOR TODAY

We are moving toward a dictatorship of relativism which does not recognize anything as definitive and has as its highest value one's own ego and one's own desires.
POPE BENEDICT XVI

WHAT GOD'S WORD SAYS

Do nothing out of selfish ambition or vain conceit, but in humility consider others better than yourselves. Each of you should look not only to your own interests, but also to the interests of others.
PHILIPPIANS 2:3-4

❚❚ PAUSE AND REFLECT

Could the contrast be any more apparent? Pope Benedict's commentary on the highest value of a dominant emerging worldview is both sobering and self-evident. It is a worldview in direct violation of Jesus' attitude as a servant leader.

Ego is defined in both positive and negative terms. Whether it is positive or negative in any given case is a function of how it relates to the Creator. When it Edges God Out, it turns into conceit and an exaggerated sense of self-importance. When it Exalts God Only, it is merely the healthy awareness of self as distinct from the world and other selves.

Fallen human nature takes its cue from Satan, the original egomaniac. Transformation is required for our egos to function properly. How is your ego functioning?

_____

_____

_____

🙏 A PRAYER FOR TODAY

Lord, thank You for Your transforming power. Thank You that I am not condemned to a life of illegitimate ego pursuits. Help me to consciously surrender my will to You each day, moment by moment as I face the heat of inevitable conflicts. Please fill me with the fruit of Your Spirit so that I can Exalt God Only. In Jesus' name, Amen!

TODAY'S TOPIC

Leader-follower relationships are characterized by clashes. So are leader-leader relationships and follower-follower relationships. And any other relationships involving human beings.

Clashes in leader-follower relationships, however, have a unique liability. Since leadership generally exists to accomplish a vision, clashes that postpone or sabotage this accomplishment are fundamentally self-defeating. The solution is servant leadership.

The true test of servant leadership begins when the EGO of the leader and the EGO of the follower engage each other. How well they recognize and overcome the pride and fear factors in their relationship determines whether they move toward mutual satisfaction of commonly held goals or share in frustrations of their own making.

The ideal, most productive relationship between leader and follower occurs when a servant-hearted leader and a servant-hearted follower engage each other in an atmosphere of mutual service and trust.

 ## LOOK INSIDE

How do you handle it when you are confronted with a self-focused learner or follower? When your leadership is challenged or your motives and methods are mistrusted? Do you do what comes naturally and resort to exerting negative, position-driven power to exert your will?

_____

_____

_____

_____

★ KEY CONCEPT

Recognizing and overcoming the pride and fear factors in a leader-follower relationship determines whether the relationship will be productive or problematic.

A POINT TO PONDER

An EGO-driven leader can create disillusionment and cynicism in even the most servant-hearted follower, resulting in an ineffective learning process.
KEN BLANCHARD AND PHIL HODGES

Could this be you? We've never seen a leader answer this in the affirmative — at least not willingly. But we've seen plenty of followers respond in the affirmative about their leaders. This suggests the difficulty of seeing unwanted truth about ourselves. So we ask again: could this be you?

NEXT STEPS

Since self-diagnosis is often mistaken, we need input from others to help us see what we can't see, what we excuse, or what we see as irrelevant.

How will you guard against being or becoming an EGO-driven leader?

Who can you go to for accurate feedback regarding EGO-driven tendencies that may develop without your awareness?

FEAR MEETS FEAR

" QUOTE FOR TODAY

No passion so effectually robs the mind of all its powers of acting and reasoning as fear.
EDMUND BURKE

 ## WHAT GOD'S WORD SAYS

Praise be to the Lord, the God of Israel, because he has come and has redeemed his people ... to rescue us from the hand of our enemies, and to enable us to serve him without fear.
LUKE 1:68, 74

▮▮ PAUSE AND REFLECT

The verses in What God's Word Says are taken from Zechariah's song. His story in the first chapter of Luke is an amazing one. *Gripped with fear* at the sudden appearance of Gabriel and stuck in disbelief of Gabriel's message, Zechariah (father of John the Baptist) was more than speechless. He was stricken dumb — unable to utter a word — for nine months, the entire time his wife, Elizabeth, was pregnant with John.

After obediently naming his newborn son John, Zechariah was released from his prison of silence. He was *filled with the Holy Spirit and prophesied* the passage we now call Zechariah's song. Notice his graduation from **gripped with fear** at the beginning of the story to *serve him without fear* in his prophetic utterance.

To what degree do fear and disbelief dog your performance as a leader? Are you able to recognize their presence and deal with them in a conscious way? Are you growing in love? ... *perfect love drives out fear* ... (1 JOHN 4:18).

🙏 A PRAYER FOR TODAY

Lord, thank You for Your love that has provided redemption for me. Thank You that it can deliver me from the fear of punishment. Thank You for releasing me to serve You and others *without fear*. Help me to grow in faith and in Your love. In Jesus' name, Amen!

 **TODAY'S TOPIC**

The four least effective relationships between a leader and follower are those in which the pride and fears of the leader and the follower commingle to create conflict, suspicion, exploitation, and isolation. Today we examine one of these four relationships: the one in which fear meets fear.

When a leader and a follower are both fearful in a relationship, they will be looking for warning signs that their fears are justified. Even initial evidence of goodwill and safety are looked on with suspicion. Negative assumptions about each other, based on stereotyping due to factors of age, race, position, ethnic background, religion and gender, can be a significant barrier to open communication.

People frequently greet these negative assumptions — and the behaviors they drive — as being personal attacks, deliberate attempts to wound. Most often, however, they are defensive moves born out of fear and ignorance. Unfortunately, regardless of the motive, they short-circuit the kind of open communication that is needed for understanding, appreciating, cooperating, and accomplishing.

Critical thinking, which begins by examining our own thinking, requires us to sort and separate facts from assumptions. Our natural tendency is to accept our assumptions as facts without even examining them for their logic or accuracy. Various kinds of fears, especially in an emotional conflict, assert themselves seamlessly into our fact base, inviting us to react outside of reason. One measure of maturity is the ability to refuse this invitation — to have enough emotional intelligence to set aside fear-based assumptions.

The arc of maturity includes graduating from the kind of fear that paralyzes us or leads us to act in self-defeating ways. This is not to say that mature leaders never again encounter this kind of fear, but they are quick to recognize it and deal with it. They have cultivated a habit of counteracting natural fear-based assumptions with carefully chosen faith-and-love-based assumptions. This allows them to greet defensive "attacks" with understanding and patience.

 **LOOK INSIDE**

What hidden assumptions are operational in your leader-follower relationships?

_____

_____

_____

_____

KEY CONCEPT

Fear meeting fear is a self-fulfilling prophecy that poisons communication and accomplishment. Although fear is a natural emotion common to all of us, we can learn to control it and gain victory over it through the exercise of critical thinking, faith and love.

A POINT TO PONDER

A leader who fears loss of position and a follower afraid of failure engage in a relationship of mutual suspicion and paralysis.

NEXT STEPS

Commit to replace fear-based assumptions with ones like these that are faith-and-love-based.

Assume the other person has good intent. (Even when the behavior or performance is bad, the intent usually is not.)

Assume a reason behind the behavior; there is a logic that seems valid to the person.

Assume the other person has legitimate needs and feelings.

Assume a long-term relationship; don't shortchange someone because you think you'll never see him again. God will make sure you do see him again — most likely in circumstances that permit poetic justice.

_____

_____

_____

_____

_____

_____

_____

QUOTE FOR TODAY

In general, pride is at the bottom of all great mistakes.
JOHN RUSKIN

WHAT GOD'S WORD SAYS

When pride comes, then comes disgrace, but with humility comes wisdom.
PROVERBS 11:2

Pride only breeds quarrels, but wisdom is found in those who take advice.
PROVERBS 13:10

PAUSE AND REFLECT

Do you want "great mistakes," **disgrace,** and **quarrels?** Not likely.
Do you want to be proud (in the negative sense of vanity)? Of course not.
Are you at risk? Absolutely.
Why? See if this Hebrew Proverb gives you a clue: **"Pride is the mask we make of our faults."**
You're probably not too excited about people seeing your faults.
Did it ever occur to you that they can't help it?

A PRAYER FOR TODAY

Lord, thank You for making me wiser than others. I enjoy having all the answers to their problems and not needing any insight from them. Please forgive me for the prideful thoughts and attitudes I have that sound so sickening when I actually put them into words. I confess my constant need for the strength of humility Jesus showed. Thank You for His incredible example. In Jesus' name, Amen!

TODAY'S TOPIC

The four least effective relationships between a leader and follower are those in which the pride and fears of the leader and the follower commingle to create conflict, suspicion, exploitation, and isolation. Today we examine another of these four relationships: the one in which pride meets pride.

When a leader and a follower both bring their pride into a relationship, it is likely to become a test of wills. Instead of proceeding through cooperation and concessions, both parties seek to promote their position by winning arguments and contests of strength. This can take an enormous toll on productivity. Thomas Jefferson stated it this way: "Pride costs more than hunger, thirst and cold."

Few leaders or followers are likely to admit bringing pride into the relationship; the greater the pride, the greater the denial. In extreme cases, organizations witness the collision of two irresistible forces. If the organization itself is fortunate enough to survive, it has to live down the legacy of two ugly epitaphs.

The antidote to pride is humility, the rarified form that goes far beyond words muttered in an acceptance speech. The form of humility we mean is the deep conviction that our perspective is limited and we need God and others. It includes the belief that authenticity is always better than posturing.

Thomas Merton said, "Pride makes us artificial and humility makes us real." Wouldn't you benefit from being real? Everyone around you would.

 ## LOOK INSIDE

Your attitude should be the same as that of Christ Jesus: Who, being in very nature God ... humbled himself (PHILIPPIANS 2:5, 8).

Think about it: If Jesus, Creator of the universe, demonstrated humility ... Jesus was not just superior in position, He was superior in nature — in every category you can name. Have you pondered the apparent absurdity of Jesus humbling Himself?

The very absurdity of the thought should be a clue to us that we have a long way to go in our understanding of humility, love, sacrifice, eternal reward — and our ability to see through the lies and deceptions of the enemy of our soul. Everything he tempts us with is some form of pride lifting itself up to God and saying, "I want my own way; I know better than you."

_____

_____

_____

_____

KEY CONCEPT

Pride meeting pride is an unproductive test of wills. We gain victory over pride through developing authentic humility.

A POINT TO PONDER

A proud founder whose company has fallen on hard times and a turnaround expert proud of his hard-nosed, trim-to-the-trunk style are likely to engage in a relationship of conflict and competition.

NEXT STEPS

Pride is a vice, which pride itself inclines every man to find in others, and to overlook in himself.
SAMUEL JOHNSON

How are you doing on the pride front? That's not a question you can answer for yourself with any authority. Who are the mirrors you can trust to give you reflections filled with both truth and grace? Do you have enough humility to ask for this kind of help? If you find it too difficult and decide to pass on it, you have your answer to the first question: failing.

PRIDE MEETS FEAR

,, QUOTE FOR TODAY

My fear, hidden from others, looms larger than life and is obvious to me. My pride, obvious to others, looms larger than my fear but remains hidden from me.
STEVE GARDNER

WHAT GOD'S WORD SAYS

Woe to you, teachers of the law and Pharisees, you hypocrites! You shut the kingdom of heaven in men's faces. You yourselves do not enter, nor will you let those enter who are trying to. Woe to you, teachers of the law and Pharisees, you hypocrites! You travel over land and sea to win a single convert, and when he becomes one, you make him twice as much a son of hell as you are.
MATTHEW 23:13-15

▌▌ PAUSE AND REFLECT

The entire chapter of MATTHEW 23 is a picture of pride meeting fear: the Pharisees abusing their authority over people. The chapter begins with Jesus upholding the positional authority of the Pharisees; they sit in *Moses' seat.* So He tells the crowd that they are obligated to do what the Pharisees teach, *but do not do what they do, for they do not practice what they preach.*

Pride often says good things, but it is filled with wrongdoing. And, of course, it either excuses or justifies its wrongdoing based on its own perverted perception of self-importance: the individual equivalent of "too big to fail."

Pride reaches its zenith in the presence of fearful followers. This is one of many truths that should cause you as a leader to constantly scrutinize the nature of your leadership and your view of those who serve you. When you fully recognize your responsibility to serve them, you move in the direction of reinforcing the humility you need to defeat pride.

_____

_____

_____

_____

🙏 A PRAYER FOR TODAY

Thank You, Lord, for exposing the truth of the liabilities hidden in my heart — my desire to exempt myself from the impossible standard I impose on others, my abuse of power to enhance my own status, my willingness to enslave followers in fear to accomplish my agenda. I confess my rationalizations, and I ask You to forgive me. Please continue to open my eyes to truth and my heart to transformation. In Jesus' name, Amen!

☀ TODAY'S TOPIC

The four least effective relationships between a leader and follower are those in which the pride and fears of the leader and the follower commingle to create conflict, suspicion, exploitation, and isolation. Today we examine another of these four relationships: the one in which pride meets fear.

When a leader interested in imposing his will and his way on the people under his control as an extension of his self-importance plays on the insecurities of the follower, the results are not likely to be for the common good.

" ... self-importance plays on the insecurities of the follower ... " This important phrase describes a dysfunctional cycle that is self-perpetuating. Prideful leaders may attract all kinds of followers, but they generally retain only two types:

- fear-dominated servants who shrink from risk and any creativity, and

- sycophants who selfishly manipulate the leader for their own ends.

Once this cycle is well established, the organization is destined for decline, much like an aging empire whose core has become rotten through dissipation.

💼 LOOK INSIDE

Do you ever see in yourself the desire to interpret the law to your own advantage? How about the tendency to become a zealot regarding one law and a cavalier regarding another?

Having enjoyed the privilege of driving on Germany's Autobahn, I have a great appreciation for its efficiency. And its speed. At home in the U.S., I find myself impatient with drivers who park in the passing lane without being in the act of passing. How dare they? Especially when I want to pass them and they are plugging up the passing lane!

Once in a great while — not nearly often enough — I see a sign instructing drivers that the left lane is for passing only. I cheer and ask myself, "Why do so many people not pay attention to that?" And I conveniently dismiss the fact that twenty times as many signs post the speed limit, which I want to treat as a mere suggestion.

What do you excuse or justify in yourself and in your leadership?

_____

_____

_____

 ## ★ KEY CONCEPT

Pride meeting fear is a leader's self-importance playing on the insecurities of the follower. We gain victory over it through our commitment to serve those we lead.

⚲ A POINT TO PONDER

An abusively proud leader and a fearful follower are likely to engage in a relationship of exploitation, resulting in a self-perpetuating performance decline.

✈ NEXT STEPS

Explore the fears of your followers. You may need to play detective or recruit the help of others to get an accurate picture of what people fear in you. This is not to suggest that the workplace should include no fear; there are healthy fears: *The fear of the Lord is the beginning of wisdom* (PSALM 111:10). What you don't want is toxic fear that can play into your natural tendency — the natural tendency for all mankind — to slip unwittingly into pride's trap.

_____

_____

_____

_____

_____

CLASSIC CLASHES BETWEEN LEADERS AND FOLLOWERS
FEAR MEETS PRIDE

QUOTE FOR TODAY

When men are ruled by fear, they strive to prevent the very changes that will abate it.
ALAN PATON

WHAT GOD'S WORD SAYS

God has said, "Never will I leave you; never will I forsake you." So we say with confidence, "The Lord is my helper; I will not be afraid. What can man do to me?"
HEBREWS 13:5-6

PAUSE AND REFLECT

The verses in What God's Word Says are the ultimate antidote for our fears.

When we examine our fears, drilling down through multiple layers by asking multiple "whys," we uncover our deepest beliefs. Sometimes they conflict with our stated beliefs. The verses above provide an excellent example of often-stated beliefs that may not be genuinely held at the deepest level. The unfortunate truth is that sometimes we think God has forsaken us. Sometimes we think He is not our helper or that His help is insufficient for our needs. Sometimes we overestimate what man can do to us.

All of these deeply held disbeliefs need to be examined in the light of God's perspective. The last few chapters of Job give great insight into the limitations of human perspective. Imagine yourself in Job's place when God says, *"Brace yourself like a man; I will question you, and you shall answer me. Where were you when I laid the earth's foundation? Tell me, if you understand"* (JOB 38:3-4).

A PRAYER FOR TODAY

Lord, thank You for Your promise that You will never leave me nor forsake me. Thank You that I need not fear the actions of others because I rest securely in Your hands. Please give me wisdom in dealing with the pride that infects those I lead — just as I am trusting You to help me deal with my own. Please increase my faith in Your ability to *work all things together for good.* In Jesus' name, Amen!

TODAY'S TOPIC

The four least effective relationships between a leader and follower are those in which the pride and fears of the leader and the follower commingle to create conflict, suspicion, exploitation, and isolation. Today we examine the last of these four relationships: the one in which fear meets pride.

When an insecure leader succumbs to making unwise concessions or tries to exert position power to gain the cooperation of a strong-willed follower, the results are damaging.

This is leadership by manipulation, and it is leadership that won't last long. If you are fear-driven and have strong-willed followers, they will not be content to continue following. If they are insubordinate or overly ambitious, they will seize the opportunity to undermine your position. If they are strong-willed but good-hearted, they are more likely to move on to a leader who is more confident and willing to take reasonable risks for worthy rewards.

Leaders in this situation must learn to face their fears in a healthy way, changing the belief system that supports their fear-based leadership. They also face the necessity of dealing with prideful followers, who need to undergo transformation or get off the bus.

LOOK INSIDE

Do you resort to position power to gain the cooperation of strong-willed followers? What fears can you identify that are in reaction to their behaviors?

_____

_____

_____

_____

If you report to someone — even if it is the chairman of the Board — do you ever respond with "malicious obedience" by complying with instructions that you know are faulty? How?

_____

_____

_____

★ KEY CONCEPT

Fear meeting pride is a leader's insecurity making unwise decisions based on the behaviors of an insubordinate follower. We gain victory over it through increased trust in the certainty of God's promises.

💡 A POINT TO PONDER

An insecure leader and a prideful, independent follower are likely to engage in a relationship of manipulation — probably a short-term relationship that never has the benefit of maturing.

✈ NEXT STEPS

Assuming that you are the leader in this fear-meets-pride equation, your surface fears are easy to identify; what lies beneath them takes more work. Uncovering the hidden (private) beliefs that compete with your stated (public) beliefs may require some help.

Often a coach or counselor can help you discover the same kinds of things in your life that you help others discover in theirs. But the fact that you can help others does not mean you can always help yourself. There is a reason for the old saying, "The man who defends himself has a fool for an attorney." The main obstacle to confronting your fears and their underlying basis is your pride.

How will you examine the hidden beliefs underlying your fears?

_____

_____

_____

_____

_____

_____

_____

CONGRATULATIONS!

Week 3 has shown you the classic clashes of leaders and followers, along with insight into preventing or resolving them. Your answers to our recurring application questions will help you move from being a hearer to a doer — someone who actually leads like Jesus.

In light of what you have learned this week:

How can you be different in your approach as a leader? As a follower?

_____

_____

_____

_____

What can you do right now — or within a week — to begin demonstrating this difference so that others can see it?

_____

_____

_____

_____

WEEK FOUR
RECOGNIZING ROOT CAUSES

MEMORY VERSE FOR THE WEEK

Christ gives me the strength to face anything.
PHILIPPIANS 4:13 (CEV)

Dealing with attitudes is tricky. Telling people to change their attitude doesn't usually produce a great deal of lasting change for a few reasons.

- Changing an attitude is hard.

- People tend to excuse their poor behavior and insist that their attitude is good.

- People sometimes don't see the correlation between their attitude and their behaviors.

The more common approach these days is to address behaviors. Because they are concrete, easily identified and measured, there is less room for debate over what is acceptable. Additionally, the independent western mind finds it easier to accept criticism of external behaviors than criticism of internal attitudes.

The problem is that behaviors are symptoms, not causes. Symptomatic treatment provides some relief but never a cure. Lasting positive change requires uncovering root causes in our belief system: beliefs that are incompatible with truth.

Uncovering hidden beliefs that are incompatible with truth is comprised of two elements:

1. Getting beneath the surface layer of our consciously held beliefs — our stated beliefs — to the beliefs that motivate actions inconsistent with our stated beliefs.

2. Knowing the truth — God's revelation — with which we want our beliefs to be compatible.

This takes help. Trying to do it yourself is similar to performing surgery on your own eye. Even if you know the procedure, it's hard to see what you're doing. God never intended us to be independent operators; that's why He created marriage, families, and the church — the body of which Jesus is the head.

This week we look at the EGO issues we are likely to face in the various learning stages. All of these can be reduced to hidden beliefs that overpower our stated beliefs. Your assignment, should you choose to accept it, is to go beyond the description of EGO issues and begin searching for the beliefs that need to change.

When you discover a faulty belief, you need to replace it with a correct belief. You can add a new belief in a moment; it's a simple conscious choice. Unfortunately, the new, correct belief is not the sole occupant of its space. The old belief still competes for dominance, challenging the newcomer's right to replace it.

This war does not usually end in a quick victory, because neither side wants to yield. The side that wins each battle is the side you strengthen through the force of your will. When your will is empowered by God's Spirit, the new, correct belief prevails and reinforces positive change.

,, QUOTE FOR TODAY

Cemeteries are full of people who thought the world couldn't get along without them.
UNKNOWN

WHAT GOD'S WORD SAYS

Let us not become conceited, provoking and envying each other.
GALATIANS 5:26

To keep me from becoming conceited because of these surpassingly great revelations, there was given me a thorn in my flesh, a messenger of Satan, to torment me. Three times I pleaded with the Lord to take it away from me. But he said to me, "My grace is sufficient for you, for my power is made perfect in weakness." Therefore I will boast all the more gladly about my weaknesses, so that Christ's power may rest on me. That is why, for Christ's sake, I delight in weaknesses, in insults, in hardships, in persecutions, in difficulties. For when I am weak, then I am strong.
2 CORINTHIANS 12:7-10

❚❚ PAUSE AND REFLECT

EGO — of the conceit variety — is a serious problem. How serious? In the Galatians verse in What God's Word Says, Paul warns us against it. Then, in the 2 Corinthians passage, he describes the extreme measures God took to prevent him from succumbing to it. The implication is that Paul — apart from God's afflicting intervention — would inevitably have become conceited. The further implication is that he would have been sidelined — unfit for service.

Whatever this affliction was, it is clear that it was no small inconvenience; it tormented Paul. His response is a model for us. Recognizing his tendency to rely on his own strength, which by eternal standards is bankrupt, he adopted a new belief: Jesus's power makes me strong especially when I am naturally weak and can claim no credit.

This belief comes neither naturally nor easily. We generally resist it all costs, which is why we are not used by God to a greater degree. Think about it: what do you really want, a temporary image or a lasting accomplishment — one that is gold, silver or precious stones in eternity because it was motivated and empowered by Jesus?

_____

_____

_____

_____

🙏 A PRAYER FOR TODAY

Lord, thank You that Your grace is sufficient to meet any need I will ever encounter. Help me to learn what it means to rely on Your strength rather than relying on the absence of adversity. Thank You that I can trust in Your power and the wisdom of Your sovereign plan. Please help me to be sensitive to my vulnerability, and help me to respond like Paul. In Jesus' name, Amen!

☀ TODAY'S TOPIC

As a leader, the quickest remedy to the EGO factor in leader-follower relationships comes from seeking to acknowledge and combat your own vulnerabilities to pride and fear. The spiritual health of the leader is the wellspring from which a follower's trust and commitment flows.

Looking for root causes in the behavior issues of your followers will often lead you to the presence of pride or fear in them. Every time you see these issues in someone else, take it as a reminder that the same issues reside in you. In ROMANS 2:1-3, Paul issues some very sound advice: *Some of you accuse others of doing wrong. But there is no excuse for what you do. When you judge others, you condemn yourselves, because you are guilty of doing the very same things. We know that God is right to judge everyone who behaves in this way. Do you really think God won't punish you, when you behave exactly like the people you accuse?* (CEV).

We don't want to imply that your coaching should not uncover wrong behaviors, attitudes or beliefs in others; this is an important part of coaching. Your attitude in doing so, however, is not to condemn but to help by shining light on what is hidden and dark. Our warning is this: as soon as you see pride in someone else, you risk the possibility of pride growing in yourself. And you will be no more likely to see it in yourself than the people you coach see it in themselves.

The good news is that whatever you prescribe for them will probably be just as effective for you. Be quick to do more than dispense good medicine; take it yourself.

LOOK INSIDE

As a follower — and we assume all leaders are followers in some relationships — you may be subject to poor treatment by an EGO-driven leader. As a follower whose self-worth and security are grounded in God's unconditional love and promises, keeping a big-picture perspective of what is to be gained or lost can truly "turn lemons into lemonade."

★ KEY CONCEPT

You, as the leader, will set the pace in dealing with EGO. Totally apart from what you preach, your ability (or inability) to detect and deal with pride and fear in yourself will motivate (or de-motivate) those who follow you. Deal with yourself first.

A POINT TO PONDER

Why do you look at the speck of sawdust in your brother's eye and pay no attention to the plank in your own eye? How can you say to your brother, 'Let me take the speck out of your eye,' when all the time there is a plank in your own eye? You hypocrite, first take the plank out of your own eye, and then you will see clearly to remove the speck from your brother's eye.
MATTHEW 7:3-5

This is one of Jesus' many statements that demonstrate His insight into the twisted behavior patterns of fallen human nature. The temptation to make this common mistake will probably never go away, but with the help of God's Spirit, you can become more sensitive to it and respond in a loving, Godly way.

NEXT STEPS

What behavior or attitude remedies have you recently prescribed for people you lead? It's very likely that even as you prescribed them, you were aware of the same problem in yourself. It may be a problem over which you've experienced significant victory, or it may be one you have yet to tackle.

Having the integrity and transparency to admit your own past and present struggles is one way to diminish the charge of hypocrisy that others might level at you — particularly if they are feeling defensive over your attention to their problem. Entering into a mutual support/accountability agreement is another possible approach. It is important not only to take the plank out of your own eye but also to communicate that you are in process and not giving yourself a free pass.

What current relationships would benefit from taking an action step in this direction?

_____

_____

_____

_____

EGO ISSUES AT THE NOVICE STAGE

" QUOTE FOR TODAY

When we are afraid, we ought not to occupy ourselves with endeavoring to prove that there is no danger, but in strengthening ourselves to go on in spite of the danger.
MARK RUTHERFORD

WHAT GOD'S WORD SAYS

Fear not, for I have redeemed you; I have summoned you by name; you are mine. When you pass through the waters, I will be with you; and when you pass through the rivers, they will not sweep over you. When you walk through the fire, you will not be burned; the flames will not set you ablaze. For I am the Lord, your God, the Holy One of Israel, your Savior ... Since you are precious and honored in my sight, and because I love you ... Do not be afraid, for I am with you.
ISAIAH 43:1-4

PAUSE AND REFLECT

Meditate for a few moments on God's promises in What God's Word Says prophesied for Israel. Since we have been grafted into Israel by faith, these promises extend to us. Careful reflection reveals that they do not imply exemption from trouble; if they did, there would be no need for the words *Fear not* and *Do not be afraid.*

The promise is that in spite of the dangers, we will be saved. And even more importantly, we are not alone. *I will be with you ... I am with you.* What more could you ask?

Whether you are the learner or the teacher in the novice stage of an undertaking, fear of failure is an EGO issue. Remind yourself that you are not alone. And the One who is with you — who has overcome every obstacle — is your source of security.

A PRAYER FOR TODAY

Lord, thank You for Your promise to be with me. Help me begin to comprehend the enormity of the simple words *with you.* In these words, You have given me the greatest promise I could ever hope for. Please forgive me when I take it for granted or fail to appreciate that it is the ultimate answer to my every prayer. Thank You that in these words You give *me the strength to face anything. In Jesus' name, Amen!*

☀ TODAY'S TOPIC

LEARNER/NOVICE EGO ISSUES	TEACHER/LEADER EGO ISSUES
• Fear of failure	• Impatience in teaching fundamentals
• Fear of inadequacy	• Frustration with slow progress
• Fear of looking foolish	• Temptation for premature delegation
• False pride in position	• Making quick judgments of potential
• False pride due to prior performance	• Fear of failure

These are formidable lists. Since we have already dealt with many of these issues, we'll touch on only a few in today's session.

Issues for the Novice

- **False pride in position:** When leaders or other competent people are learning a new skill, they inevitably look like novices in that skill. For some, this is more than embarrassing; they see it as a threat to the dignity of their position. Obviously, this impedes their progress.

- **False pride due to prior performance:** This is a cousin to the position problem; it is also related to looking foolish. People accustomed to performing at a high level may be embarrassed by their initial awkwardness and be tempted to quit — especially if they had unrealistic expectations at the outset.

Issues for the Leader

- **Frustration with slow progress:** This can be a simple warning to back off on an inflated sense of self-importance and entitlement that have crept into your hidden beliefs. It might also signal a need to reevaluate your priorities. Should someone else be responsible for teaching this person at this level, or should you realign your priorities to raise the value of developing people over accomplishing tasks? What is most strategic for you in the long run? Make a carefully considered choice and coach yourself into allowing your feelings to align with your beliefs and decisions.

LOOK INSIDE

We can't overemphasize the need for you to identify the learning stage you are in with regard to your various roles and skills. Knowing the issues in each stage helps keep you ahead of them.

I am a Novice in _____ and my issues are likely to be _____

_____

_____

 ## KEY CONCEPT

If you are growing, you are a novice in some area of development. Novices need someone to help them over early failures and successes so they can get a longer-term view that builds stability. Leaders of novices primarily instruct.

 ## A POINT TO PONDER

The labels — Novice, Apprentice, Journeyman, and Master — are all task specific. Communicating this clearly helps learners who are competent in other areas accept that they are novices in a new area, subject to novice characteristics and frustrations while they are simultaneously masters in the other areas.

NEXT STEPS

Identify those who are in the novice stage of a specific task in which you are coaching them.

_____ is a Novice in _____

_____

_____ is a Novice in _____

_____

_____ is a Novice in _____

_____

How will you adjust in these situations to make your coaching more effective?

_____

_____

_____

_____

_____

_____

_____

_____

EGO ISSUES AT THE APPRENTICE STAGE

" QUOTE FOR TODAY

Great works are performed not by strength, but by perseverance.
SAMUEL JOHNSON

WHAT GOD'S WORD SAYS

Jesus replied, "No one who puts his hand to the plow and looks back is fit for service in the kingdom of God."
LUKE 9:62

Being confident of this, that he who began a good work in you will carry it on to completion until the day of Christ Jesus.
PHILIPPIANS 1:6

❚❚ PAUSE AND REFLECT

Consider the bookends these verses represent. The first is a warning regarding the seriousness with which God views perseverance in the service of His kingdom. The second is an encouragement that despite our failures, God provides what we need to persevere. How does this affect your approach to learning? Your approach to teaching?

_____

_____

_____

_____

A PRAYER FOR TODAY

Lord, thank You for providing what I need when I need it so that I can honor You with my life. Thank You for Your patience and mercy in dealing with me. Help me as a teacher and coach to exhibit Your qualities — the fruit of Your Spirit — in the way I look at people and problems. Help me not to confuse the two. Thank You for Your example in the Scriptures as well as in my own life. In Jesus' name, Amen!

☼ TODAY'S TOPIC

LEARNER/APPRENTICE EGO ISSUES	TEACHER/LEADER EGO ISSUES
• Discouragement with lack of progress	• Fear of failure
• Impatience with the learning process	• Frustration with lack of enthusiasm
• Loss of faith in the learning process	• Unrealistic expectations of people
• Fear of failure	• Fear of the opinion of others
• Fear of inadequacy	• Fear of criticism
• Loss of faith in the leader	• Fear of loss of position
• Diminished enthusiasm for the task	

Issues for the Apprentice

- **Loss of faith in the learning process:** When faced with repeated failures in some part of a task, learners may lose faith that they are capable of performing it. A teacher's encouragement can overcome this, but continued failures may tempt them to lose faith in the process or even the leader. They may forget that most skill development consists of two steps forward and one step back — sometimes one forward and two back.

  It is possible that an improvement in the learning process might speed the journey toward proficiency, but unrealistic expectations need to be addressed. If learners believe that "normal" progress is much faster than what they can manage, the temptation to quit becomes difficult to resist.

Issues for the Leader

- **Frustration with lack of enthusiasm:** Great satisfaction accompanies coaching enthusiastic, capable learners. It's less satisfying but not difficult to be patient with enthusiastic, less-capable learners. The assumption is that they are applying themselves at a high level — really trying to integrate your insights and directives. But it's much harder to deal with reluctant learners, those who seem to lack motivation.

This is where one of the greatest skills of leadership comes into play. If you can recognize that lack of motivation is often caused by a feeling of hopelessness or unworthiness, you can tilt your emotions more toward empathy than impatience. Inspiration may be the lacking ingredient: you need to supply a combination of casting the vision for what can be and offering confidence that it will be. When the learner is low on faith, you can loan some of yours.

- **Fear of criticism:** A cousin to fear of failure, this severely limits what you attempt. Herbert Bayard Swope said "I cannot give you the formula for success, but I can give you the formula for failure: try to please everybody."

Jesus never made this mistake. He was unlike anyone who ever walked the planet in His singular devotion to pleasing an audience of One. Caring only for what the Father cared about, no criticism — even from the religious elite — could dissuade Him.

 ## LOOK INSIDE

We can't overemphasize the need for you to identify the learning stage you are in with regard to your various roles and skills. Knowing the issues in each stage helps keep you ahead of them.

I am a Apprentice in _____ and my issues are likely to be _____

_____

_____

_____

 ## KEY CONCEPT

If you are growing, you are an apprentice in some area of development. Apprentices, having passed through the excitement of a new interest, now face the challenge of commitment. As the leader/coach, don't give in to the temptation to do tasks rather than delegate simply because you can do it better and faster. Just as the apprentice needs to commit, you need to be committed to growth and development. Praise successes. Ask learners to review and analyze where things went wrong.

A POINT TO PONDER

The work will teach you how to do it.
ESTONIAN PROVERB

You learn to lead by leading. You learn to write by writing. You learn to sing by singing. You learn to quit by quitting. Some conceptual, abstract learners are relatively content with spouting principles they never apply. Don't be one, and don't allow it in those you are coaching. Get elbow deep in the application, the action, the work itself; it will make the instruction come alive.

NEXT STEPS

Identify those who are in the apprentice stage of a specific task in which you are coaching them.

_____ is an Apprentice in _____

_____

_____ is an Apprentice in _____

_____

_____ is an Apprentice in _____

_____

How will you adjust in these situations to make your coaching more effective?

_____

_____

_____

_____

_____

_____

_____

EGO ISSUES AT THE JOURNEYMAN STAGE

❞ QUOTE FOR TODAY

We are more often frightened than hurt; and we suffer more from imagination than from reality.
MARCUS ANNAEUS SENECA

WHAT GOD'S WORD SAYS

Do not be afraid of those who kill the body but cannot kill the soul. Rather, be afraid of the One who can destroy both soul and body in hell. Are not two sparrows sold for a penny? Yet not one of them will fall to the ground apart from the will of your Father. And even the very hairs of your head are all numbered. So don't be afraid; you are worth more than many sparrows.
MATTHEW 10:28-31

‖ PAUSE AND REFLECT

Fear is not the exclusive domain of novices — or any other stage; it shadows our entire lives. In What God's Word Says, Jesus tells us once to be afraid and twice not to be. The difference, of course, is the nature and object of our fear. Isn't it fascinating that He would tell us to fear God and then follow that statement with one of the strongest declarations in the Bible about God's love and care for us? This conviction is why Jesus never swerved from playing for an audience of One. Whom do you fear? To whom are you playing?

🙏 A PRAYER FOR TODAY

Thank you, Lord, for loving us completely in spite of knowing us intimately. We rejoice to know that nothing is hidden from You and yet You tell us not to fear. Thank You that our value to You is based on Your righteousness and not ours. May we live in Your luxurious grace as we learn to fear You and no one else. In Jesus' name, Amen!

 **TODAY'S TOPIC**

LEARNER/JOURNEYMAN EGO ISSUES	TEACHER/LEADER EGO ISSUES
• Fear of failure when moving into new situations	• Lack of sensitivity to loss of enthusiasm
• Fear of success in expanded use of skills	• Overuse of competence
• Burnout — loss of enthusiasm and vision	• Fear of intimacy required to deal with the individual issues
• Fear of obsolescence	• Fear of criticism
• Fear of competition	• Fear of the learner surpassing the teacher
• Fear of confronting slips in performance	

Issues for the Journeyman

- **Fear of obsolescence, competition, and confronting slips in performance:** Although these fears differ in many ways, they have at least one thing in common: all of them are made less threatening through a commitment to ongoing training and growth. Any journeyman who thinks he has finally arrived and can autopilot his way through a task, role, or career, has justifiable fear.

Issues for the Leader

- **Fear of intimacy required to deal with the individual issues:** This fear is common to transactional leaders who do not place a high enough value on the importance of the relationships they foster with those they lead. It can stem from an actual fear of intimacy: I am afraid of being known (transparent) — or it can be time related: I can't afford the time it would take to know you well enough to be effective with you. Both beliefs are faulty and need to be replaced.

 **LOOK INSIDE**

We can't overemphasize the need for you to identify the learning stage you are in with regard to your various roles and skills. Knowing the issues in each stage helps keep you ahead of them.

I am a Journeyman in _____ and my issues are likely to be _____

_____

_____

⭐ KEY CONCEPT

If you are growing, you are a journeyman in some area of development. Leaders of journeymen who assume their work is done when learners have become proficient enough to be sent out on their own, neglect them at their peril. Journeymen need to be nurtured and appreciated or they can become disillusioned and toxic in their impact on the people around them.

💡 A POINT TO PONDER

The journeyman with an audience of One has a firm foundation. *Therefore everyone who hears these words of mine and puts them into practice is like a wise man who built his house on the rock. The rain came down, the streams rose, and the winds blew and beat against that house; yet it did not fall, because it had its foundation on the rock* (MATTHEW 7:24-25).

In adversity, the journeyman on a firm foundation still experiences fear, but her fears melt like the sandy foundation of the foolish man.

📬 NEXT STEPS

Identify those who are in the journeyman stage of a specific task in which you are coaching them.

_____ is a Journeyman in _____

_____

_____ is a Journeyman in _____

_____

_____ is a Journeyman in _____

_____

How will you adjust in these situations to make your coaching more effective?

_____

_____

_____

_____

_____

_____

_____

_____

_____

EGO ISSUES AT THE MASTER/TEACHER STAGE

" QUOTE FOR TODAY

The bigger a man's head gets, the easier it is to fill his shoes.
UNKNOWN

WHAT GOD'S WORD SAYS

So, if you think you are standing firm, be careful that you don't fall.
1 CORINTHIANS 10:12

Perseverance must finish its work so that you may be mature and complete, not lacking anything.
JAMES 1:4

❚❚ PAUSE AND REFLECT

The perseverance James is talking about is persevering through trials and the testing of your faith. One of the greatest trials for a leader — particularly one who gains public acclaim — is the challenge to remain humble. Humility and servant leadership are inseparable, and joy is their offspring. This is the wisdom of God's pride-busting plan.

The statement, "God has a plan for your life" is true but incomplete. God has a plan for your life as a *part of His kingdom plan.* He has a plan for your service, and the joy you will find is in the serving. Are you finding it? If not, consider whom you are serving.

🙏 A PRAYER FOR TODAY

Lord, thank You for the way You coach me, using the right amount of testing and encouragement to develop my trust in You in the times when I don't feel Your presence. Please protect me from complacency, arrogance, and misuse of skills. Help me to keep my eyes on You so I don't give in to fears of competition or obsolescence or loss of control. I'm trusting You in Jesus' name, Amen!

TODAY'S TOPIC

LEARNER/MASTER EGO ISSUES	TEACHER/LEADER EGO ISSUES
• Complacency with current knowledge of skills • Unwillingness to take criticism or direction • Arrogance • Misuse of skills for self-serving purposes	• Fear of personal competition from the fully inspired and equipped follower • Fear of personal obsolescence when the learner can do what you do • Unwillingness to share information or recognition • Fear of loss of control

Issues for the Master/Teacher

- **Complacency with current knowledge of skills:** This has probably been an issue for millennia, but its danger has never been as great as in today's high pace of technological innovation. Although the latest is not always the greatest, upgrading your knowledge is necessary to discern the difference.

Issues for the Leader

- **Unwillingness to share information or recognition:** This is clearly tied to the fears that precede it in the list. It indicates a reversion to self-serving behavior, the opposite of what got you to this point. It's always a temptation, whether you're hoarding resources and credit to get ahead or to stay ahead, but it puts the focus on the wrong goal. Reread the two verses in today's What God's Word Says.

LOOK INSIDE

We can't overemphasize the need for you to identify the learning stage you are in with regard to your various roles and skills. Knowing the issues in each stage helps keep you ahead of them.

I am a Master in_____and my issues are likely to be _____

_____

_____

★ KEY CONCEPT

You are a master in some areas. Masters face their own set of vulnerabilities as they release, assign, and empower others to do what they have been doing. Continue being a Master servant leader.

💡 A POINT TO PONDER

No one appreciates the value of constructive criticism more thoroughly than the one who's giving it.
UNKNOWN

If you're not mature enough to take criticism, you're too immature for praise.
UNKNOWN

Your response to criticism is both an indicator of maturity and a potential early-warning system for the pride that inevitably pries its way through the door of accomplishment. How are you responding these days?

_____

_____

_____

_____

✈ NEXT STEPS

Identify those who are in the master stage of a specific task in which you are coaching them.

_____ is a Master in _____

_____ is a Master in _____

_____

_____ is a Master in _____

_____

How will you adjust in these situations to make your coaching more effective?

_____

_____

_____

_____

_____

CONGRATULATIONS!

You've reached the end of this study. We want to cheer you across the finish line by encouraging you to answer our two application questions. Remember: it's not just the theory you know but how you apply and practice it that helps you become someone who leads like Jesus.

In light of what you have learned this week:

How can you be different in your approach as a leader? As a follower?

_____

_____

_____

_____

What can you do right now — or within a week — to begin demonstrating this difference so that others can see it?

_____

_____

_____

AFTER WORDS

Ken's wife, Margie, once remarked that the gap between knowing and doing is greater than the gap between ignorance and knowledge. It is also a harder gap to close because it requires a willingness to go public with changes in behavior that may be resisted, resented or look foolish in the eyes of others. When the task at hand is providing spiritual leadership to others, having the right heart motives and the right thinking can become fuzzy sentimentalities if they are not translated into action. It is by the work of your hands that you will demonstrate to others the state of your heart.

Jesus got His hands dirty fulfilling His promise to make His disciples into *"fishers of men."* He committed His personal time and energy to a step-by-step transformational process as He instructed, coached, mentored and finally commissioned these future leaders. In His final hours before going to the Cross, Jesus counted teaching His disciples until they understood (JOHN 17:7-8) as one of the ways He had glorified His Father during His time of earthly ministry. He calls all that would follow Him to offer up their hands to His use and purpose so that they may also glorify their heavenly Father. May the work of your hands in the guidance and encouragement of others give witness to the nature of your servant heart!

THE AUTHORS

ABOUT THE AUTHORS

KEN BLANCHARD

Few have impacted the day-to-day management of people and companies more than Ken Blanchard. As a prominent author with over three dozen books including *The One Minute Manager*, speaker and business consultant, Ken is universally characterized as one of the most insightful, powerful and compassionate men in business today. Speaking from the heart with warmth and humor, he is a polished storyteller who makes the seemingly complex easy to understand.

With a personal faith in Jesus Christ, Ken recognizes and lifts up Jesus as the greatest leadership role model of all time. He co-founded The Center for Faithwalk Leadership, now known as *Lead Like Jesus*, in 1999 with a mission "to glorify God by inspiring and equipping people to lead like Jesus."

Ken, his wife, Margie, two adult children, and three grandchildren live in Southern California. He is the co-founder, with his wife, Margie, and Chief Spiritual Officer of the Ken Blanchard Companies. With a Ph.D. from Cornell University, he has been a college professor, an imaginative entrepreneur, and a much sought after business guru. He is an avid golfer and a friend to many!

PHIL HODGES

Phil Hodges, co-founder of *Lead Like Jesus*, served as a human resource and industrial relations manager in corporate America for 36 years with Xerox Corporation and U.S. Steel. In 1997, he served as a Consulting Partner with The Ken Blanchard Companies where he had responsibilities in leadership and customer service programs.

In addition to helping leaders of faith walk their talk in the marketplace, Phil developed a passion for bringing effective leadership principles into the church when he served as member and chairman of his local church elder council for more than ten years. Phil finds great joy in his life-role relationships as husband, father and grandpa.

In 1999, Phil co-founded *Lead Like Jesus* whose mission is "to glorify God by inspiring and equipping people to Lead Like Jesus." He is the co-author of five books including *Lead Like Jesus: Lessons*

from the Greatest Leadership Role Model of All Time and *The Most Loving Place in Town: A Modern Day Parable for the Church*, with Ken Blanchard. Phil and his wife, Jane Kinnaird Hodges, live in southern California where they are involved daily in their happiest season of influence as parents and grandparents in their expanding family.

STEVE D. GARDNER

A writer and corporate trainer investing in leaders with a dream team of collaborators at Ambassador Enterprises in Fort Wayne, IN are just a few things Steve does day to day. After graduation from Wheaton College, he and his wife, Maria, spent 28 years touring five continents in a music ministry that included writing and recording 16 albums.

As vice-president of Emerging Young Leaders, Steve began writing and editing leadership mentoring books including *Successful Youth Mentoring* (Volumes I and II) and *Lead On*. He has since written curricula used around the world by Crown Financial Ministries and has either ghosted or assisted in the writing of approximately 20 books.

A lover of tennis, skiing and scuba, Steve tells Ken he's saving golf for his golden years. In the meantime, he and Maria enjoy performing occasional concerts and spending time with their three grandchildren.

LOOKING FOR YOUR
NEXT STEPS?

CEO or teacher, pastor or parent, shopkeeper or student —
if you desire to impact the lives of others by leading like Jesus,
we invite you to join the LLJ movement and expand your leadership
abilities. Lead Like Jesus offers leadership-building resources for
teens and young adults as well as for seasoned executives, all
with the goal of demonstrating God's love for people while
helping them change the way they live, love, and lead.

The following products are available for purchase at
www.LeadLikeJesus.com

SIGN UP TO RECEIVE THE
E-DEVOTION

*You can receive a new Lead Like Jesus
devotional three times a week in your
inbox! These brief, insightful and
challenging reflections will help you
lead more like Jesus. Sign up at
www.LeadLikeJesus.com today!*

**CONTINUE YOUR PERSONAL
GROWTH BY PURCHASING**
LLJ STUDY GUIDES

*Containing personal reflections, memory
verses, prayers, activities, and guidelines
for creating your own leadership plan.
These study guides contain lessons for
anyone who aspires to lead like Jesus.*

ENGAGE THE NEXT GENERATION THROUGH
STUDENT RESOURCES

*Learning to lead like Jesus is an ongoing
pursuit. LLJ materials for students
are designed to foster life-changing
leadership habits and develop skills
early that will last a lifetime.*

**PARTICIPATE IN A
HIGH-IMPACT WORKSHOP**
ATTEND AN
ENCOUNTER

*An interactive program,
Encounter helps leaders
create positive change in
both their personal and
professional relationships.*

**INCREASE YOUR PERSONAL
GROWTH THROUGH**
ACCELERATE™

*Accelerate™ combines written
content, video, and powerful
questions to foster continued
growth as a LLJ leader. An
online program delivered daily
and built to move at a speed
that's right for you.*

LEAD LIKE JESUS